To the children of Bramalea Church of Christ.

Levi was a girl in the second grade.
Every autumn, she looked forward to the
"Fall Fair" because she loved playing all the
carnival games and going on the fun rides.

One day at school, while Levi was walking to her class, she saw a big poster that read: "Fall Fair Opens Friday."
She was so excited to go home and tell her parents.

The moment she got home, she put down her backpack and ran to tell her parents.
"Mom, Dad, the Fall Fair is coming Friday! Can we please go?"

"Honey, you're going to have to go with Dad. I have to take your brother to his soccer game," said Mom.

"I'd love to take you," replied Dad.

That Friday, Levi and her dad were lining up at the ticket booth to enter the Fall Fair.
"I'm going to get you a wristband so we can go on all the rides and play the games," said Dad.

Levi could hardly contain her excitement. "Just make sure to stay with me and hold my hand. This place has a lot of distractions, and I don't want you to get lost."
"Sure thing, Dad," replied Levi.

Once they got their wristbands, they were on their way. As they entered the fair, Levi noticed the beautiful lights on all the rides. She could hardly hold her dad's hand because she was so eager to go on everything.

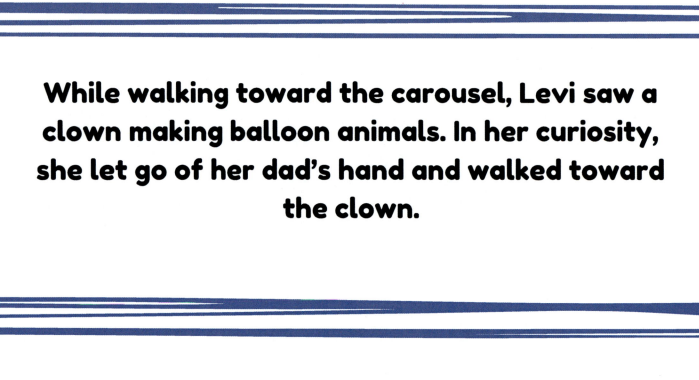

While walking toward the carousel, Levi saw a clown making balloon animals. In her curiosity, she let go of her dad's hand and walked toward the clown.

After getting her balloon, she turned back and suddenly realized her dad was not there. The carnival seemed so much bigger now that she was alone.

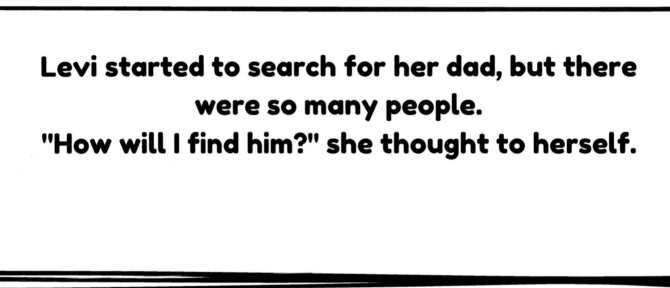

Levi started to search for her dad, but there were so many people.
"How will I find him?" she thought to herself.

Levi began to feel afraid. It was so busy and loud. She walked toward the House of Mirrors. "Maybe I'll find my dad there," she said.

As she made her way, she heard a faint noise in the distance that sounded like her dad's voice. She tried to follow the noise but did not see her dad.

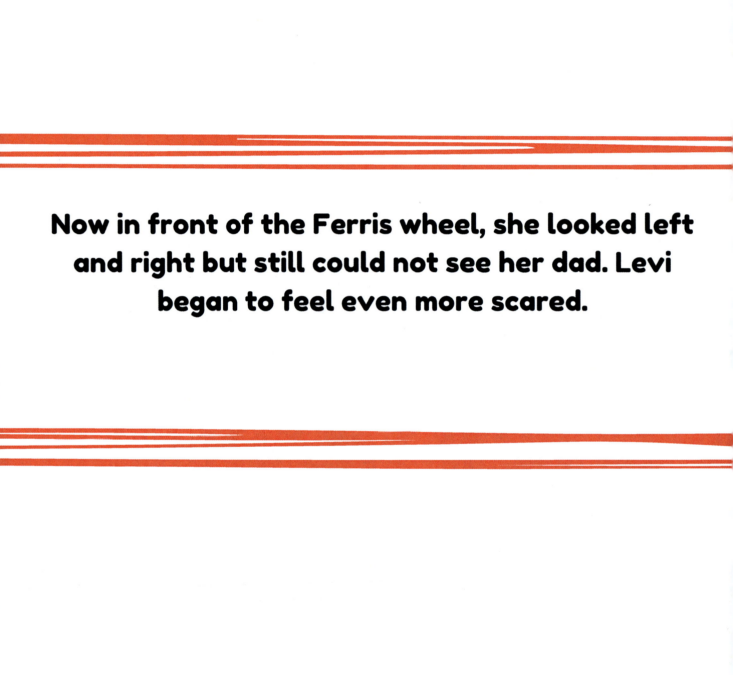

Now in front of the Ferris wheel, she looked left and right but still could not see her dad. Levi began to feel even more scared.

Then, in the distance, she heard, "Levi, where are you?" This time it was a bit clearer, and she could tell it was her dad's voice calling her.

After running for a few minutes, trying to follow her dad's voice, Levi found herself in front of a haunted house. It was spooky and loud. Feeling very scared and thinking she might not find her dad, Levi closed her eyes and started to cry. "Why did I let go of my dad's hand?" she said to herself. "Now I'm lost."

While tears ran down her cheeks, she suddenly heard her dad's voice calling her. Turning back, she opened her eyes, and there, in the midst of the crowd, she saw her dad.

Levi ran as fast as she could and hugged her dad tightly.

While tears ran down her cheeks, she said, "Dad, I promise to never let go of you like that again."

"I'm happy you heard my voice calling you," replied Dad.

On the ride home, Levi's dad said, "What happened today reminded me of the words of Jesus, when he said, 'My sheep hear my voice, and I know them, and they follow me.'"

"Levi, in life, you're going to face many distractions trying to get you to let go of God's hand. Today, you learned what can happen when you let go—you can find yourself lost and in a scary situation. But if you ever find yourself lost and scared, listen for God's voice and follow it."

"Jesus says that if we follow His voice, He will give us eternal life, and nothing can ever snatch us away from Him."
That day, Levi learned a lesson she would never forget: that God would never stop calling her, even if she was lost. Most importantly, if she listened to His voice and followed Him, nothing could ever take her away from Him.

1- How can I hold on to God?

The Bible says: "He who began a good work in you will bring it to completion" (Philippians 1:6). When God enters your heart, He doesn't just leave you. His Spirit remains at work in you, and although you will sometimes fail, the Spirit of God helps you hold on to Him.
So how can you hold on to God? It starts with trusting that God is never going to leave you, and through that trust, God will strengthen you so that no matter what you may face, you will not face it alone.

2- How can I hear God's voice?

Imagine you're on a game show where the challenge is to identify the impostor based on their voice. The host blindfolds you, and two people step forward to speak—one is a stranger, and the other is someone you know very well.
Do you think you'd be able to tell who the impostor is? Of course, right? But why? Because you recognize the voice of the person you know. You've spent time with them, talked with them often, and built a relationship.
Jesus said, "My sheep listen to my voice; I know them, and they follow me" (John 10:27). If you want to hear God's voice, build a relationship with Him. Talk to Him through prayer, and in time, you'll recognize His voice—because you know Him.

3- What should I do if I feel lost?

The Bible says: Psalm 119:105 - "Your word is a lamp to my feet and a light to my path." In life, there will be times when you may feel lost. But you are not alone. You can ask God's help for guidance, and you can read His word for understanding. But there's one more thing you can do—you can find friends who can help you. For example, at church, there are many people who can support you, and help you during hard times.
God wants you to be among His people. Why? Because we are meant to be a community united for Him. Together, we are stronger!

Manufactured by Amazon.ca
Bolton, ON